Celebrate
Valentine's Day

Carolyn Otto
Consultant, Dr. Jack Santino

NATIONAL GEOGRAPHIC
WASHINGTON, D.C.

love

On February 14th, we celebrate Valentine's Day with love, cards, and candy. This celebration of friendship and affection, of sweethearts and love, goes far back in time.

∧ An old-fashioned valentine

cards

candy

< A girl sends a heartfelt message to her mother.

∧ A heart-shaped box of chocolate candies

Throughout the ages, there have been many festivals on or around February 14th. These celebrations marked the very beginning of spring, the promise of warmer weather to come, and the awakening of flowers and crops and all things that grow.

∧ It is said that swans choose their mates for life. On Lake Geneva, Switzerland, these two come together to form a perfect heart.

> A Valentine's Day parade makes its way through a crowded street in the Philippines.

We welcome springtime.

People often think of Valentine's
Day as a time for weddings. This tradition
probably goes back to St. Valentine.

There are many stories about him.
One legend says he was a priest or bishop.
He was put to death on February 14th,
around the year 270.

Will you marry me?

∧ *Amanda Hughes and Matthew Self skate into marriage during a Wedding On Ice celebration in Chicago.*

< *Newlyweds travel in style on passenger-sized tricycles in Bangkok, Thailand.*

Why? The emperor of Rome, Claudius II, decided that men made better soldiers if they were not engaged or married. But St. Valentine went against the emperor's wishes. In secret, the priest continued to perform the marriage ceremony for people in love.

It is said that St. Valentine wrote a letter before he died. He signed it: "From Your Valentine." Some people think this was the first valentine.

A couple greets a snowy
Valentine's Day in Finland
with a sparkling heart.

> In the Philippines, a woman shows the valentine heart she made.

We make valentines.

∧ A selection of modern store-bought cards

In Europe, during the Middle Ages, the custom of sending valentine greetings to friends and loved ones on February 14th became common.

Valentine cards were beautiful then, hand-made and hand painted—sometimes with real gold. Some were edged with lace and decorated with dried and pressed flowers.

We still like to make beautiful valentines today. We use foil and stickers. We use white lacy doilies and lots of colored paper.

We buy cards and

It was an American who began to sell valentine greetings on a bigger scale. In the mid-1800s, Esther A. Howland set up shop in her father's stationery store. Her valentine cards were so popular that she had to ask her friends to help assemble them.

∧ A card made by Esther Howland.

> Sweethearts pick out balloons in Amman, Jordan.

< In Iraq, a young woman shops for Valentine's Day flowers.

flowers and balloons!

Love, crazy love.

∧ *Couples scream, but somehow manage to make their wedding vows while upside down on a roller coaster of love at Busch Gardens in Tampa, Florida.*

Sometimes we do wacky, crazy things for love. We get married in big groups or on a ski slope. We send our love an underwater message: "Please marry me!"

> *A bride and groom hit the slopes after their mountaintop wedding ceremony in Loveland, Colorado.*

< *In an aquarium in Shanghai, China, a diver delivers a valentine message that translates to "Li Simin, please marry me!" Li Simin accepted.*

Love at first sight.

We decorate our houses

and classrooms and shops with hearts and cupids.

In legend, Cupid is known as the son of Venus, the ancient Roman goddess of love. Cupid might look like a baby with wings, but he can shoot powerful arrows of love at men, women, boys, girls— even other gods and goddesses.

< *Cupid shoots water instead of arrows in this golden fountain at Linderhof Palace, in Bavaria, Germany.*

Once shot by one of Cupid's arrows, a person falls in love with whoever is in sight.

> *Cupid awaits a Valentine's Day delivery in Los Angeles, California.*

On Valentine's Day we

wear red clothes. We deliver our valentines to the people we care about. We start with our families. Then we might sneak a valentine into a neighbor's mailbox or slip a greeting card under a friend's door.

∧ *Dressed all in red for the occasion, Emily Main of Los Angeles, California, finishes up the last of her Valentine's Day greetings.*

> *Carolyn Crystal Chan (on left) gives a free hug to a woman in Singapore.*

We tell people they are special!

∧ *Twelve-year-old Dani Decker of Manitowoc, Wisconsin, writes a Valentine's Day message to a soldier in Iraq.*

We let people know we like them. We let them know that they have made a difference to us. We make them laugh when we surprise them or give them funny valentines.

Using her classroom's homemade mailbox, a girl in California sends a valentine greeting to a classmate.

At school we put our valentines into a big box or in specially decorated envelopes. We give valentines to our principals, our teachers, and all of our classmates—just about everyone we know.

We sometimes have a secret Valentine. We make special cards for our secret Valentine, but we don't sign them. We give out hints. We want them to guess who we are, but we don't want to make it too easy.

Do you have a secret Valentine?

∧ Candy hearts

Some of us have parties.

When it comes time to open our valentines, we read each one. It's exciting. Sometimes the cards are silly, sometimes sweet.

We have fun and

eat sweet things.

We play games. We dance. And we eat sweet things. We eat chocolates, cookies, and frosted cupcakes with colorful sprinkles. We eat candy hearts that say things like: "Be Mine," "New Love," "Hug Me," "Kool," "Only You," or "Luv Ya!"

∧ Decorated cupcakes send loving messages.

< In Burlington, Iowa, seniors and kids participate in a Valentine's Day sock hop.

Sometimes we put candy hearts with our cards and send sweet greetings.

A man in the Netherlands expresses joyous love with outstretched arms and a bouquet of flowers.

> *A Kenyan woman prepares red roses to sell in her shop for Valentine's Day.*

We send flowers.

On Valentine's Day we might give people small gifts as well. We give flowers, especially roses. But we also give daffodils, forget-me-nots, tulips, and other flowers.

For hundreds of years, people have used flowers to say what their hearts feel. Red roses mean true love. Pink roses are for friends. Lilacs are for your first love. A dandelion says "You make me happy!"

Love, sweet love.

On Valentine's Day, we celebrate
love. We give sweet things to our friends
and family. We think of those who are
close to us. We have fun!

High in the Swiss Alps,
a couple embraces
after an exhausting
Valentine's climb.

MORE ABOUT VALENTINE'S DAY

Contents

Just the Facts

WHO CELEBRATES IT: Valentine's Day is mostly celebrated in Great Britain, France, Canada, the United States, and Mexico. However, the holiday has also become popular in many other countries.

WHAT: A holiday to celebrate love, friendship, and affection.

WHEN: February 14.

RITUALS: Making and sending valentine cards. Decorating our homes and classrooms, and dressing in red. Making cookies and pink frosted cupcakes and good things to eat.

FOOD: Sweets! Cookies, cakes, cupcakes, candy, and chocolate!

Musical Valentines Game

This game is like musical chairs, but instead of using chairs, you use hearts.

WHAT YOU WILL NEED:
scissors, red construction paper, music

1. Cut out large hearts from red construction paper. You'll need one fewer than the number of players.

2. Tape the hearts to the floor in a large circle.

3. When the music starts, everyone walks outside of the hearts, as in musical chairs.

4. When the music stops, each person has to stand on one of the hearts. But whoever does not make it to a heart is not out. Instead, the other kids call to that person and say, "You can be my valentine!" The person chooses someone to share a heart with.

5. Remove one heart from the floor each time the music stops.

6. As there are fewer hearts, it gets harder to fit part of your foot onto a paper heart, so remember to be gentle as everyone tries to fit onto the last few hearts!

Celebrating Love Around the World

People celebrate love and friendship in different ways and on different days all over the world.

In Japan, women give chocolate, flowers, or candy to friends, co-workers, and sweethearts on February 14th. On March 14th, men are supposed to return the favor . . . only they give white chocolate.

In China, there is a holiday called Qi Xi, or The Night of the Sevens. It falls on the seventh day of the seventh lunar month on the Chinese calendar. Young women throw a sewing needle into a bowl of water. If the needle floats, it is believed that the girl will find a sweetheart.

Long ago, European women would write their sweethearts' names on paper and roll them into balls of clay. They put the clay into a bowl of water. The first bit of paper that floated to the surface would bear the name of a woman's true sweetheart.

In Denmark, would-be couples exchange valentine greetings signed with a line of dots. Each dot represents a letter in the sender's name. If the person who receives the greeting figures out the name from the dots, he or she sends a candy egg to the friend at Easter.

v *Sweethearts perch high atop elephants in a group wedding ceremony in Ayutthaya province, Thailand.*

Great-Grandmother's Sugar Cookies

FOR DECORATING:
Colored sugar, ready-made frosting, icing in a tube, or candy sprinkles

YOU WILL ALSO NEED:
Wax paper, rolling pin, heart-shaped cookie cutter or plastic knife, cookie sheet, spatula

I n my great-grandmother's Kansas town, she was famous for her sugar cookies, which are old-fashioned and not too sweet. If you don't want to make the dough, you can always buy ready-made refrigerated sugar cookie dough in your supermarket, roll the dough flat, and cut out the heart shapes. Bake according to the package directions and have fun decorating your Valentine's Day cookies. Whichever way you make them, get an adult to help you.

INGREDIENTS:
½ cup brown sugar
½ cup white sugar
½ cup shortening or softened unsalted butter
1 egg
1 teaspoon vanilla
½ cup sour milk (to make the milk sour, add a teaspoon of white vinegar to ½ cup milk)
3½ cups flour
1 teaspoon baking powder
½ teaspoon baking soda
½ teaspoon salt

1. Wash your hands.
2. Put the brown sugar, white sugar, shortening or butter, egg, and vanilla into a large bowl and mix with a spoon.
3. Stir in the sour milk and mix until thick.
4. In a separate bowl, mix the flour, baking powder, baking soda, and salt.
5. Add the flour to the sugar mixture, a little at a time. Mix with a wooden spoon. When it gets too thick, use your hands.
6. Refrigerate the cookie dough for about one hour to make it easier to work with.
7. Preheat the oven to 375°F.
8. Lay a sheet of wax paper on the counter. Put the cool dough on the paper and use the rolling pin to flatten it, making it about ¼-inch thick.
9. Cut out heart shapes with a cookie cutter or by hand with a knife.
10. You can sprinkle sugar on the cookies now or decorate them after they are cooked. Bake them for about 10 minutes or until they are light brown on the edges.
11. The cookies will be hot! Carefully use a spatula to put them on paper or a rack.
12. Once the cookies cool, invite your friends to help decorate them. Have a good time!

Find Out More

BOOKS

Those with a star (*) are especially good for children.

Butler, Father Alban. *Lives of the Saints*. Benziger Brothers, Inc. New York, 1995.

*de Groat, Diane. *Roses Are Pink, Your Feet Really Stink*. Harper Trophy, 1997. Gilbert finds that it's hard to write nice valentine poems for the not-so-nice kids in his class. A lighthearted book with a serious message.

Griffin, Robert H., and Ann H. Shurgin, editors. *The Folklore of World Holidays*, 2nd edition. Gale Research, 1999. This is a big research book that you should be able to find in your library. It has lots of information and is fun to read.

*Hurd, Thacher. *Little Mouse's Big Valentine*. HarperCollins, 1990. A sweet story about a mouse who makes a valentine heart that's so big he has trouble finding someone who will take it.

Kull, A. S. *Secrets of Flowers*. Stephen Greene Press, 1972. This is a charming, old-fashioned book.

The New Larousse Encyclopedia of Mythology, with an introduction by Robert Graves. Crown Publishers, 1989. Another big library book; you can read about Cupid and Venus here.

WEB SITES

Plenty of Web sites have fun activities for kids. You can go to Ask.com or Wikipedia.org and follow the links. The best sites I found were:

www.history.com/minisites/valentine This is a really fun site, with video clips and lots of information about the history of Valentine's Day.

wikipedia.org/wiki/Valentine's Day This page gives a good overview of the holiday and has links to related topics.

www.dltk.holidays.com/Valentines This site has fun holiday activities for kids.

holidays.kaboose.com Look under "Holidays" for Valentine's Day.

Ask.com I used this site to find out about Esther Howland. You will find a lot of fascinating facts there.

< *Bryant Davis peeks into his Valentine's Day envelope in Webster Groves, Missouri.*

Glossary

Cupid: Cupid is a Roman god from long ago. The Greeks called him Eros. He is most often pictured as a child, but he has a bow and arrows. His arrows make people fall in love.

Doilies: Doilies used to be made of cotton or linen, usually crocheted. Today they are often made of paper, cut carefully to look like real lace.

Heartfelt: A word used when something is "felt from the heart."

Middle Ages: Used to describe the time period in European history from about 500 to 1500.

Stationery: Paper for writing on, especially paper and matching envelopes for writing letters; a stationery store might sell paper, pens, and other items related to writing.

Sweethearts: Sweethearts are people in love. They do sweet things for each other.

Venus: The ancient Roman goddess of love, thought to be very beautiful. Cupid was often referred to as her son.

Vow: A pledge or solemn promise.

Where This Book's Photos Were Taken

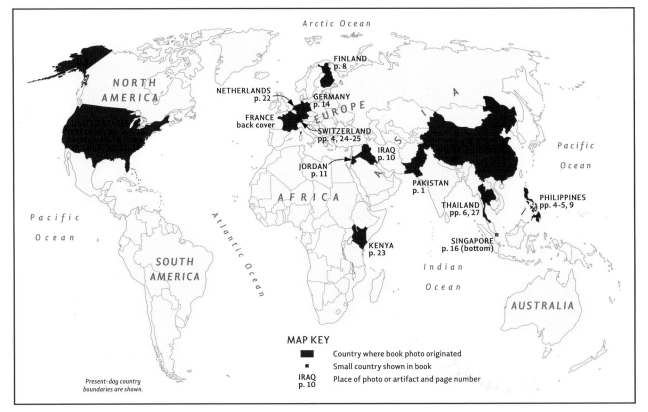

MAP KEY

■ Country where book photo originated
▪ Small country shown in book
IRAQ p. 10 Place of photo or artifact and page number

Present-day country boundaries are shown.

Valentine's Day: For Love and Custom

by Jack Santino

For a day that is supposed to celebrate love, Valentine's Day generates mixed feelings. It is denounced by some, despised by others, and dreaded by many. Like a few other holidays on the American calendar, Valentine's Day is plagued by the twin curses of social pressure and commercialization. But despite what many people believe, Valentine's Day is not a recent invention of the greeting-card or floral industry. In fact, it was mentioned in medieval literature, as well as by William Shakespeare.

Geoffrey Chaucer provides an early mention in his "Parliament of Fowls" (here, updated from Middle English): "So this was Saint Valentine's Day, / When every fowl cometh there to choose his mate." We can see from this passage that Valentine's Day was already associated with love and with choosing one's mate. The day was also connected to the cycles of nature, as it was said that turtledoves chose their mates on that day.

Valentine's Day was also once associated with the return of hibernating animals and migrating birds. In fact, our Groundhog Day tradition is derived from this custom, and traces of the connection between the two (now separate) holidays still exist. In Michigan, for instance, February 14 is locally known as Bear Day—bears being the most prominent of the emerging hibernators. In Missouri, Groundhog Day is still sometimes celebrated on the 14th of February, rather than on the 2nd.

The larger theme is our connection to the cycles of nature—an awareness of the fertility of the earth, and the love and fertility of humans, as spring nears. Throughout the ancient world and into the Middle Ages, festivals celebrating love, the creatures of the earth, and the flowers of the season were held during early spring and late winter. The Romans had the Floralia, during which couples were paired together, and Europeans had their winter carnivals and masquerades. With the coming of Christianity, these holidays became the carnivals of Mardi Gras, prior to Lent, and the masked balls of Valentine's Day.

Writing hundreds of years after Chaucer, Shakespeare provides more information about old Valentine's Day customs. In *Hamlet*, Ophelia sings:

Good morrow! 'tis Saint Valentine's Day
All in the morning betime.
And I a maid at your window
To be your Valentine.

This passage alludes to the ancient belief that the first person you would see on Valentine's Day was destined to be your true love.

In the 18th and 19th centuries, British children chanted rhymes on Valentine's Day. Today, however, children are more likely to give mass-produced cards to their schoolmates. Yet even the valentine card has a long history. As early as 1415, the Duke of Orleans, captured in battle and held at the Tower of London, sent his wife in France a love poem for Valentine's Day. The first stanza of his poem, "To Dorinda, on Valentine's Day," reads: "Look how, my dear, the feather'd kind, / By mutual caresses joyn'd / Bill, and seem to teach us two / What we to love and custom owe."

Today the holiday has been mercilessly commercialized by those industries that profit from it. But if we see past all the commercialism and realize the central ideas at the base of this celebration—that at the end of a long winter there will be spring, flowers, warmth, and love; that we are a part of the natural cycle of life, much as the birds, bears, and groundhogs are; that in celebrating love we are celebrating life. If we interpret Valentine's Day in this way ourselves, we may realize how much we too owe to love and custom.

Jack Santino

Jack Santino is a professor of folklore and popular culture at Bowling Green State University in Ohio. He has written several books on holidays, celebrations, and rituals, including All Around the Year: Holidays and Celebrations in American Life.

For Ross

PICTURE CREDITS

Front Cover: © David Branch/Tyler Morning Telegraph/Associated Press; Back cover: © Serra Antoine/Corbis Sygma; Spine: © Lori Sparkia/Shutterstock; 1: © Ilyas Dean/The Image Works; 2: © JLP/Jose L. Pelaez/Corbis; 3 (top): © Fine Art Photographic Library: London /Art Resource: NY; 3 (bottom): © Edyta Linek/Shutterstock; 4: © Martial Trezzini/Keystone/Associated Press; 4-5: © Paul Souders/WorldFoto/Robertstock.com; 6: © Sukree Sukplang/Reuters; 7: © Tim Boyle/Getty Images; 8: © Jyrki Komulainen/Nordic Images/Getty Images; 9 (top): © Pat Roque/Associated Press; 9 (bottom): private collection; 10: © Samir Mizban/Associated Press; 11 (top): from the private collection of Vivian Krug/ www.EmotionsCards.com; 11 (bottom): © Hussein Malla/Associated Press; 12: © Jim Tuten/ Busch Gardens/Associated Press; 13 (top): © Sean Cayton/The Image Works; 13 (bottom): © str/Associated Press; 14: © Adam Woolfitt /Corbis; 15: © Stock Connection/ FotoSearch; 16 (top): © Nicole Katano/ Brand X; 16 (bottom): © Nicky Loh/ Reuters; 17: © Sue Pischke/ HTR/Associated Press; 18-19: © Michael Newman/ PhotoEdit Inc; 20 (top): © bluestocking/ Shutterstock; 20 (bottom): © John Lovretta/The Hawk Eye/ Associated Press; 21: © Bo Zaunders/Corbis; 22: © Benelux/ zefa/Corbis; 23: © Sayyid Azim/Associated Press; 24-25: © Brian Harris/ZUMA Press; 27: © Piyamon Sukplang/ Reuters; 28: © Andrew Keegan and Mary Beth Oelkers-Keegan; 29: © Liz Streeter/ Associated Press.

Text copyright © 2008 Carolyn Otto.
All rights reserved. Reproduction of the whole or any part of the contents without written permission from the National Geographic Society is strictly prohibited.

Library of Congress Cataloging-in-Publication Data
Otto, Carolyn.
  Celebrate Valentine's Day / Carolyn Otto ; consultant, Jack Santino.
    p. cm. — (Holidays around the world)
Includes bibliographical references and index.
ISBN 978-1-4263-0213-8 (trade : alk. paper) —
ISBN 978-1-4263-0214-5 (library : alk. paper)
1. Valentine's Day. I. Title.
GT4925.O77 2007
394.2618—dc22

            2007033764

Series design by 3+Co. and Jim Hiscott. The body text in the book is set in Mrs. Eaves. The display text is Lisboa.

Front cover: In Tyler, Texas, Darnicia Hendricks enjoys a rare snowfall while holding Snuggles, her Valentine's Day teddy bear.
Back cover: Children use their hands to sign "I love you" in front of the Mur de Je t'aime, a wall with a message in Paris, France. The words "I love you" are written on the wall in hundreds of languages.

Title page: A Pakistani man sells heart-shaped balloons on Valentine's Day.

Founded in 1888, the National Geographic Society is one of the largest nonprofit scientific and educational organizations in the world. It reaches more than 285 million people worldwide each month through its official journal, NATIONAL GEOGRAPHIC, and its four other magazines; the National Geographic Channel; television documentaries; radio programs; films; books; videos and DVDs; maps; and interactive media. National Geographic has funded more than 8,000 scientific research projects and supports an education program combating geographic illiteracy.

For more information, please call 1-800-NGS LINE (647-5463) or write to the following address:
National Geographic Society
1145 17th Street N.W., Washington, D.C. 20036-4688 U.S.A.

Visit us online at www.nationalgeographic.com/books

For information about special discounts for bulk purchases, please contact National Geographic Books Special Sales: ngspecsales@ngs.org. For rights or permissions inquiries, please contact National Geographic Books Subsidiary Rights: ngbookrights@ngs.org

PUBLISHED BY THE NATIONAL GEOGRAPHIC SOCIETY

John M. Fahey, Jr., *President and Chief Executive Officer*
Gilbert M. Grosvenor, *Chairman of the Board*
Nina D. Hoffman, *Executive Vice President; President, Book Publishing Group*

STAFF FOR THIS BOOK

Nancy Laties Feresten, *Vice President, Editor-in-Chief of Children's Books*
Bea Jackson, *Design and Illustrations Director, Children's Books*
Amy Shields, *Executive Editor, Children's Books*
Jennifer Emmett, *Senior Editor*
Mary Beth Oelkers-Keegan, *Project Editor*
Lori Epstein, *Illustrations Editor*
Melissa Brown, *Project Designer*
Carl Mehler, *Director of Maps*
Priyanka Lamichhane, *Assistant Editor*
Rebecca Baines, *Editorial Assistant*
Katelin Sanford, *Photography Intern*
Rachel Armor, *Editorial Intern*
Jennifer A. Thornton, *Managing Editor*
Gary Colbert, *Production Director*
Lewis R. Bassford, *Production Manager*
Maryclare Tracy, Nicole Elliott, *Manufacturing Managers*
Susan E. Borke, *Senior Vice President and Deputy General Counsel*

ACKNOWLEDGMENTS

Many thanks to Jack Santino for his advice and his honest and knowledgeable note. Thanks to Nancy for her longtime friendship. To our teacher friends go glorious hugs for a rewarding and difficult job. A special note of gratitude to Patti Soderberg, who let us know about the Musical Valentines game. And to the "Sages" group in Colorado Springs, who helped me decorate cookies.